Now the band that inspired that great saying, "Stop the music!"

In the style that has become synonymous with the name Henny Youngman, this collection brings us the great comic's all-time hit list: 500 uproariously funny one-liners.

I came home last night, by accident, and there's the car in the dining room. I said to my wife, "How did you get the car in the dining room?"
She said, "It was easy. I made a left turn when I came out of the kitchen."

Henny's style has been imitated by many, but few can come close to his superb wit and jocularity.

My wife is so neat. In the middle of the night I went to the kitchen for a drink. When I got back I found the bed made.

JACKIE IS WACKY!

You've roared at his riotous radio antics! You've howled at his hilarious record albums and videos! You've died laughing dialing his X-rated telephone party line! He's Jackie "The Joke Man" Martling, America's favorite vulger jokesman! And now you can get your hands on the very finest in bawdy buffoonery when you order a big bunch of this rib-tickling top banana's gut-busting best from Pinnacle Books!

RAUNCHY RIDDLES   (17-072-3, $2.95)

MORE RAUNCHY RIDDLES   (17-073-1, $2.95)

THE ONLY DIRTY JOKE BOOK   (17-074-X, $2.95)

JUST ANOTHER DIRTY JOKE BOOK (17-075-8, $2.95)

Henny Youngman's

500

All-Time Greatest One-Liners

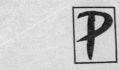

PINNACLE BOOKS
WINDSOR PUBLISHING CORP.

PINNACLE BOOKS

are published by

Windsor Publishing Corp.
475 Park Avenue South
New York, NY 10016

Ninth printing: August, 1990

Printed in the United States of America

CONTENTS

Henny Youngman's
500 All-time Greatest
One-liners

Henny's
Introductions

1.

INTRODUCTIONS

Here's a man who spends most of his time in the barber shop . . . reminiscing.

* * *

Barbers don't charge him for cutting his hair. They charge him for searching for it.

* * *

He dresses like an unmade bed!

* * *

He doesn't have an enemy in the world. He's outlived them all.

He was the only man ever kicked out of the Army for looking like a one-man slum.

* * *

I understand you throw yourself into everything you undertake. Please go and dig a deep well.

* * *

Here's a real musician. He was born with a fiddle in his hands and a bow in his legs.

* * *

Each of these boys is a soloist in his own right. If you don't believe me, listen to them when they try to play together.

* * *

Now the band that inspired that great saying, "Stop the music!"

A group that actually made a record. The only reason it didn't sell is that they forgot to put a hole in the middle.

*   *   *

The leader comes from a family with a turn for music. They were organ grinders.

*   *   *

As a conductor, he doesn't know his brass from his oboe.

*   *   *

What an ad libber! He couldn't even have an argument with anyone without a Tele-Prompter.

*   *   *

As a comedian he has a repertoire of six jokes all told, and told, and told.

I won't say that [name] is fat, but when she got married they needed three relatives to give her away.

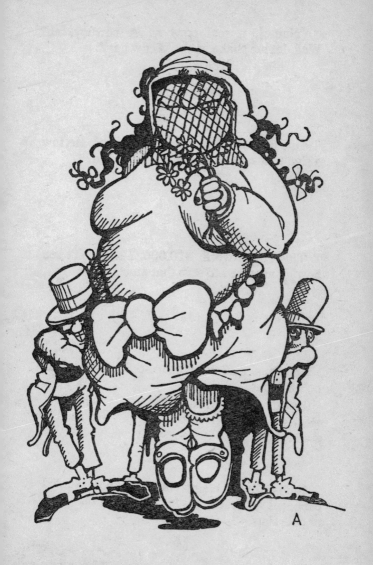

A

[Name], a real cowboy. A cowboy, eh? Well, let me shake your old cow hand.

* * *

One of those dogs can actually read. He saw a sign that said "Wet Paint" and he did.

* * *

This dog is worth $10,000. I still don't see how he managed to save that much.

* * *

Here's a fastidious couple. She's fast and he's hideous.

* * *

[Name] who claims that he once planted cabbages and razor blades and got a fine crop of cole slaw.

16

[Name], a big-hearted girl with hips to match.

* * *

When they heard [name] was being honored, everybody, as one, shouted, "Why?"

* * *

Much has been written and said about [name], and he is here tonight to deny it.

* * *

[Name] has got more talent in his little finger than he has in his big finger.

* * *

[Name] is so full of alcohol that if anyone gives him a hot-foot he'll burn for three days.

Our next entertainer needs no introduction. He needs an act.

* * *

[Name] used to go to school with his dog. But one day they were separated. His dog graduated.

* * *

[Name] isn't exactly backward, but he once bought a toothbrush and asked if it came with directions.

* * *

[Name] is the only man I ever met with a seersucker face.

* * *

[Name] is the perfect example of what happens if you take an overdose of Geritol.

[Name] was chosen Miss America when she was 16. Of course, there were very few Americans in those days.

* * *

[Name] has found real happiness. Her boyfriend likes her husband.

* * *

[Name] looks like a million, but nobody can be that old.

* * *

[Name] must have Egyptian blood in her. Every time I try to kiss her she says, "Tut, tut."

* * *

[Name] thinks himself a wit, and he's probably half right.

[Name] admits he uses old jokes. He says think of them as folk humor.

I

[Name] is really not a midget. He's a Texan with the wind let out of him.

* * *

[Name] lives alone but occasionally he goes out in a crowd for a little change.

* * *

Let's give the next act a big reception. You see they need the money and they are too embarrassed to collect unemployment insurance.

* * *

Next we have an act that is rapidly becoming an institution, which is where it belongs.

* * *

Our next performers have become so rich in show business that even their garbage is gift-wrapped.

[Name] has such a big mouth he can eat a banana sideways.

* * *

[Name] is so old that he remembers when toothpaste was white.

* * *

[Name] doesn't drink, smoke, or chase women. In fact, Lloyd's of London once gave six-to-one that he was dead.

* * *

[Name] is so full of bull that cows follow him home.

* * *

[Name] once resigned from a job as governess because the children were too backward and the father was too forward.

[Name] says she doesn't want to get married because she has got cold feet. I can't think of a better reason.

* * *

[Name] has been married so many times that she doesn't get a new license each time any more. Now, they just punch the old one.

* * *

[Name] has a figure like a leopard . . . good in spots.

* * *

[Name] is a brunette by nature . . . but a blonde by Clairol.

* * *

[Name] is a bachelor girl . . . crazy about bachelors.

[Name] had some trying experiences in Hollywood. At least five producers kept trying.

* * *

[Name]'s motto is "Love thy neighbor." His neighbor is an 18-year-old hooker.

* * *

You can write the story of [name]'s life on a piece of confetti.

* * *

[Name]'s last audience was real polite. They covered their mouths when they yawned.

* * *

[Name] was a pioneer on television. He was the first to be turned off.

* * *

[Name] is an M.C. all right . . . a Mental Case.

[Name]'s approach to love and romance is soft music, soft breezes, soft lights, and soft soap.

* * *

[Name] is frank and earnest with women. In Fresno he's Frank and in Chicago he's Ernest.

* * *

[Name] prefers a girl who's sexy, not brainy. He says when he feels intellectual, there's always the public library.

* * *

[Name] is a slick operator. He never gives a girl enough rope to make a marriage knot.

* * *

At a very early age, [name] showed signs of belonging to the theatre. He put gum under the seat of his high chair.

[Name] was born to the stage. His first grade teacher picked up his option after twenty-six weeks.

* * *

[Name] would look perfect in something long and flowing . . . say a river.

* * *

I'm sorry to announce we have two disappointments tonight. Robert Redford couldn't make it, and [name] could.

* * *

[Name] only goes out with girls who wear glasses. He breathes on the lenses so they can't see what he's doing.

* * *

[Name]'s been losing his mind. He recently received a letter warning him. "Stop playing around with my wife, or I'll kill you!" The letter was unsigned.

[Name] only goes out with girls who know all about the birds and the bees . . . and the pill.

* * *

[Name] wants to be remembered . . . by anybody.

* * *

[Name's] last show was closed after three performances on account of bad language . . . by the critics.

* * *

When you talk about [name] there are two things you must mention: humility and modesty. Because those are the two things he doesn't have.

* * *

[Name] took singing lessons for six months and did so poorly the teacher made him give them back.

Ladies and gentlemen, I am not going to bore you with a speech today, but I will present to you a man who will: [name].

* * *

[Name] also does magic. Last night he disappeared with the host's wife.

* * *

[Name]'s last audience was with him all the way. No matter how fast he ran, he couldn't shake them.

* * *

What an entertainer! When [name] performs, the nightclub waives the amusement tax.

* * *

Insults

2.

INSULTS, IN CASE YOU
NEED THEM

You'll make money someday. Your ignorance is comical.

* * *

When you get up in the morning, who puts you together?

* * *

My wife can find a corner in the middle of the block.

* * *

Last time I saw you, you were in a nightmare.

If there's never been a suicide in your family, why don't you break the monotony?

* * *

I bet you have no more friends than an alarm clock.

* * *

He's got a tongue and it's not only for sarcasm.

* * *

You have a ready wit. Let me know when it's ready.

* * *

If you ever need a friend, buy a dog.

* * *

If you were alive, you'd be a very sick man.

* * *

Why don't you freeze your teeth and give your tongue a sleigh ride?

I'd like to say we're glad you're here. I'd like to say it.

* * *

I'll bet your parents hit the jerk-pot.

* * *

Why don't you go and scrap your fat?

* * *

There's only one thing that keeps me from breaking you in half: I don't want two of you around.

* * *

If there's ever a price on your head, take it.

* * *

Show me a Jewish boy who doesn't go to medical school and I'll show you a lawyer.

* * *

He was born at home but when his mother saw him she went to the hospital.

He spends money like water: drip, drip, drip.

* * *

I once insulted a witch doctor and he's my curse.

* * *

I'd put a curse on you, but somebody beat me to it.

* * *

I know this man through thick and thick.

* * *

I looked high and low for you. I didn't look low enough.

* * *

He's a real good egg, and you know where eggs come from.

* * *

Show me a man with very little money and I'll show you a bum.

Are you naturally stupid or did a Cuban hijack your brain?

* * *

You look like a talent scout for a cemetery.

* * *

Four drunks looked at him. They took the pledge.

* * *

Someday you'll go too far, and I hope you'll stay there.

* * *

He's hoping for a lucky stroke—his rich uncle's.

* * *

At least he gives his wife something to live for: a divorce.

* * *

May we have the pleasure of your absence?

What got you out of the woodwork?

* * *

I can't forget the first time I laid eyes on you . . . and don't think I haven't tried.

* * *

I'm going to name my first ulcer after you.

* * *

Why don't you step outside for a few years?

* * *

Why don't you go to a window and lean out too far?

* * *

He was born on April 2nd—a day too late.

* * *

I know you have to be somebody, but why do you have to be you?

* * *

I never forget a face, and in your case I'll remember both of them.

You appear to be as happy as if you were in your right mind.

* * *

It's good to see you. It means you're not behind my back.

* * *

You know I'd like to send you a Valentine, but I haven't figured out how to wrap lace around a time bomb.

* * *

You're the kind of person I would like to have over when I have the measles.

* * *

Was the ground cold when you crawled out this morning?

* * *

I remember you. You're a graduate of the Don Rickles Charm School.

* * *

Sit down, you make the place look shabby!

I'm paid to make an idiot out of myself. Why do you do it for free?

*　*　*

If they can make penicillin out of moldy bread, surely they can make something out of you.

*　*　*

Don't move. I want to forget you just the way you are.

*　*　*

If I were you, I'd return that face to Abbey Rents.

*　*　*

Are you naturally stupid or are you waiting for a brain transplant?

*　*　*

I don't believe in reincarnation, but what were you when you were alive?

He has more crust than a pie factory.

* * *

He doesn't get ulcers, he gives them.

* * *

He should have been an undertaker. He has no use for anyone living.

* * *

Some people bring happiness wherever they go. You bring happiness whenever you go.

* * *

There's a pair of shoes with three heels.

* * *

Look at him, sex takes a holiday.

* * *

You remind me of some of those new dances: one, two, three, jerk.

41

Zsa Zsa Gabor has been married so many times she has rice marks on her face.

* * *

Mickey Rooney has been married so many times he has a wash-and-wear tuxedo.

* * *

He had a nightmare last night. He dreamed that Dolly Parton was his mother and he was a bottle baby.

* * *

Let me tell you about our guest of honor. Never has a man been more sworn at, more spit at, more maligned, and rightfully so.

* * *

There's one good thing about being bald: It's neat.

* * *

How can you talk all night without stopping to think?

You have a nice personality, but not for a human being.

*　*　*

Look, I'm not going to engage in a battle of wits with you. I never attack anyone who is unarmed.

*　*　*

I'd like to introduce you to some friends of mine. I want to break off with them.

*　*　*

Is your family happy? Or do you go home at night?

*　*　*

I wish somebody would kidnap you. But who would they contact?

*　*　*

Someday you'll find yourself and will you be disappointed.

I like you—I have no taste—but I like you.

* * *

When the grim reaper comes for you he'll have a big smile on his face.

* * *

There's a guy who lives alone and looks it.

* * *

Do me a favor. On your way home, make it a point to jaywalk.

* * *

I'd like to run into you again . . . sometime when you're walking and I'm driving.

* * *

His friends don't know what to give him for Christmas. What do you give a guy who's had everybody?

44

If Moses had known you, there would positively have been another commandment.

*   *   *

The more I think of you the less I think of you.

*   *   *

He lights up a room when he leaves it.

*   *   *

What do you give a guy who has nothing?

*   *   *

Why don't you sit down and rest your brains?

*   *   *

Lots of people owe a lot to him: ulcers, nausea, diarrhea.

Don't sell him short. In college he was a four-letter man and they called him bleep.

* * *

I love that man. Very few people know this man was born an only twin.

* * *

He was a real gentleman. He reminds me of Saint Paul, one of the dullest towns in America.

* * *

The things he does for his friends can be counted on his little finger.

* * *

We don't want to make this afternoon too long. Our guest of honor has to get home because this is the night he gets his annual urge . . . and his wife gets her annual headache.

The last time he was in a hospital, he got get well cards from all the nurses.

* * *

To Johnny Carson. "Johnny, was that suit made to order?"
"Yes."
"Where were you at the time?"

* * *

To Milton Berle. Milton, you have the Midas touch. Everything you touch turns into a muffler.

* * *

To Dean Martin. Dean, if you had your life to live over again, do it overseas.

* * *

Just got back from Mexico. I was appearing there at the Kaopectate Festival. Wish I knew how to spell it. I made a run for it.

I'm planning to invite you to my party. There's always room for one more bore.

*   *   *

There's a train leaving in an hour. Be under it!

*   *   *

I think the world of you . . . and you know what condition the world is in today.

*   *   *

There's only one thing wrong with you. You're visible.

*   *   *

If you'll stop telling lies about me I'll stop telling the truth about you.

I don't know what makes you tick, but I hope it's a time bomb.

* * *

Next time you give your clothes away, stay in them.

* * *

Why don't you start neglecting your appearance? Then maybe it'll go away.

* * *

I enjoy talking to you. My mind needed a rest.

* * *

It's nice hearing from you. Next time send me a post card.

* * *

Cultural
Quirks

3.

CULTURAL QUIRKS

A sign saying "Jesus saves." Underneath it somebody wrote, "Moses invests."

* * *

Camp Hiawatha, Camp Seneca—that's where the Jewish kids go for the summer. Camp Ginsberg is where the Indian kids go.

* * *

What is the difference between a regular shark and a Puerto Rican shark?
The Puerto Rican shark has two gold teeth.

* * *

We just found out why Golda Meir turned down the Suez Canal. No boardwalk!

St. Patrick's has a drive-in confessional. You toot and tell.

* * *

Indian girl marries Jewish boy. They have to give their new son a name to please both sides of the family. They name him "Whitefish."

* * *

Jewish man talking to his friend: "If I live I'll see you Tuesday. If I don't, I'll see you Wednesday."

* * *

What do you call a Jewish baby who isn't circumsised?
A girl!

* * *

Why does the Italian Navy have glass-bottomed boats?
So they can see the old Italian Navy!

A Polish guy locked his keys in his car. It took him over an hour to get his wife out.

* * *

A man pulls up to a policeman in Israel and asks, "Say, can I park here?"

The policeman says, "No."

So the man asks, "How about these other cars?"

The policeman says, "They didn't ask!"

* * *

Polish fella bought himself a pet zebra. Called it Spot.

* * *

Polish Jigsaw Puzzle: one piece.

* * *

Some guy bought 1,000 garbage trucks. He's selling them to the Polish people as condominiums with escalators.

Two Polish guys with burnt faces. They were bobbing for French fries!

* * *

They sent the Polish terrorist to blow up a car. He burnt his lips on the exhaust pipe!

* * *

They have a new Polish mime group. They talk!

* * *

The Polish Dracula bit Dolly Parton on the neck!

* * *

They taught a Polish guy how to run a helicopter. It's up 800 feet. All of a sudden it falls to the ground. I said to him, "What happened?"

He says, "It got chilly up there. I turned off the fan."

I love the Italian people. During World War II an Italian girl saved my life. She hid me in her cellar. It was on Mulberry Street!

* * *

A hold-up man walks into a Chinese restaurant, says, "Give me all your cash."
The Chinaman asks, "To take out?"

* * *

Did you hear about the Polish pyramid club? They won 52 pyramids.

* * *

There's a new Norwegian insurance policy. It's called "My Fault Insurance."

* * *

A Norwegian appeared with five other men in a rape case police line-up. As the victim entered the room, the Norwegian blurted, "Yep, that's her!"

Why don't Norwegians play hide and seek?
'Cause nobody wants to find them!

* * *

How do Norwegians spell "farm?"
"E-I-E-I-O"

* * *

Why did the Norwegian freeze to death?
Because he went to the drive-in movie to see
"Closed for the Winter."

* * *

What did the Norwegian call his cocktail of
Vodka and Milk of Magnesia?
"A Phillips Screwdriver."

* * *

Did you ever see one of those Italian mov-
ies, "Bread, Love and Pizza" or "Bread, Love
and Mozzarella?"
What are all the lovers over there, bakers?

I just bought a little Italian car. It's called a "Mafia." There's a hood under the hood.

* * *

When I go to Israel, in Milton Berle's honor, I will have a tree uprooted.

* * *

This Irish guy dropped dead. Who should tell the wife, and how? A guy volunteered. He knocked at the door, a lady came out, and he said, "Is this the widow Ryan?"

"I'm not the widow Ryan."

"Wait until you see what they're dragging in the back door."

* * *

A bomb fell on Italy and slid off.

* * *

Psychiatrist. A Jewish doctor who can't stand the sight of blood.

There's an elegant synagogue in Beverly Hills. On Yom Kippur they close for the Jewish Holidays!

* * *

Two Jewish ladies were in a building. One says to the other, "Do you see what's going on in the Middle-East, Iran, and Spain?"

"I don't see anything. I live in the back of the building."

* * *

Two Jewish women in the building. One says to the other, "Did you hear there is a rapist in the building?"

She says, "Yes, I know. I already gave!"

* * *

Let's face it, the American businessman is in a tight spot. Whenever he comes up with something new, the Russians invent it a month later and the Japanese make it cheaper!

It's good to read "Dear Abby" now and then. What with Russia and Red China and the H-bomb, it's wonderful to know there are still some people in this world whose biggest worry is how they should acknowledge a wedding present.

* * *

This Russian roulette craze is really getting around. I understand Alcoholics Anonymous has its own version. They pass six glasses of tomato juice around, and one of them is a Bloody Mary.

* * *

It's one of those British science fiction pictures. You can tell it's British because the Martians all carry umbrellas.

* * *

You look at the news—strikes, bombings, muggings—and sometimes you wonder, maybe the Indians should have had stricter immigration laws.

Did you read about the new Broadway nightclub that's run by Indians? And what a gimmick! They charge you $24 for a Manhattan!

* * *

This cancer scare is getting so bad, Indians are smoking filtered peace pipes.

* * *

I hear they're putting up a $20,000,000 hotel right in the heart of Moscow. Gonna call it the "Comrade Hilton."

* * *

No wonder the Russians are getting so confident. If they've been watching television, they must figure every American has tired blood, indigestion, or nagging headaches!

* * *

Marital
Bliss

4.

MARITAL BLISS

Man takes his boss home for dinner. A woman lets them in. Boss says, "Is that your wife?"

He says, "Would I marry a maid that ugly?"

* * *

My wife is in the Olympics. She's a javelin catcher.

* * *

Vasectomy means never having to say you're sorry.

* * *

I just discovered a new birth control device. My wife takes off her make-up.

My wife is so neat. In the middle of the night I went to the kitchen for a drink. When I got back I found the bed made.

*   *   *

One word you never hear in my house is divorce. Murder yes, but divorce, no.

*   *   *

Jaws reminds me of my wife. She avoided being bitten by a shark. She opened her mouth first.

*   *   *

Dentist who was having a romance with one of his married woman patients said to her, "Darling, we've got to stop seeing each other, you're down to your last tooth!"

*   *   *

My wife will buy anything marked down. She brought home two dresses and an escalator.

*   *   *

My wife wanted a foreign convertible. I bought her a rickshaw.

A woman shot her husband with a bow and arrow. She didn't want to wake up the kids.

* * *

My wife and I had an argument. She wanted to buy a fur coat. I wanted to buy a car. We compromised: bought a fur coat and kept it in the garage.

* * *

You ought to see my wife in a bathing suit. She's bow-legged and I'm knock-kneed. When we stand together we spell the word "ox."

* * *

I bought my wife a new foreign cookbook and now she claims she can't get parts for the meals.

* * *

Payday at my house is like the Academy Awards. My wife says, "May I have the envelope please?"

* * *

When my wife asked me to start a garden the first thing I dug up was an excuse.

My wife and I were considering a divorce, but after pricing lawyers we decided to buy a new car instead.

* * *

My wife had a fight with her mother so she's coming home.

* * *

I haven't talked to my wife in three weeks. I didn't want to interrupt her.

* * *

I took my wife to a wife-swapping party. I had to throw in some cash.

* * *

My wife has a new recipe for an exotic gourmet dinner: "First take two credit cards . . ."

* * *

My wife called me. She said, "There's water in the carburetor."
I said, "Where's the car?"
She said, "In the lake."

My wife saw the garbagemen leaving our house. She shouted, "Am I too late for the garbage?"

They answered, "No, jump in!"

* * *

My wife is in Miami. She talks so much her tongue is sunburned!

* * *

Do you know what mixed emotions are?

It's when you see your mother-in-law drive over a cliff in your new Cadillac!

* * *

My wife should have been a lawyer. Every time we have an argument and she feels she's losing, she takes it to a higher court—her mother!

* * *

Now she's on a diet. Coconuts and bananas. She hasn't lost any weight. *But can she climb a tree!*

* * *

She's tried Metrical, safflower oil—now she eats nothing but garlic and Limburger cheese. Nobody can get near her, so from a distance she looks thin.

I've been married for fifty years and I'm still in love with the same woman. If my wife ever finds out, she'll kill me.

*   *   *

Valentine's Day she gave me the usual gift. She ate my heart out!

*   *   *

I said to my mother-in-law, "My house is your house." Last week she sold it.

*   *   *

My wife went to the beauty shop and got a mud pack. For two days she looked nice. Then the mud fell off.

*   *   *

In Hollywood they have community property. A couple gets divorced, she gets the Jaguar, he gets the little cap.

*   *   *

My mother-in-law is so nearsighted she nagged a coat hanger for an hour.

My wife likes those little foreign cars. I bought her two: one for each foot.

* * *

I miss my wife's cooking—as often as I can.

* * *

Bought my wife a car. Three weeks ago she learned how to drive it. Last week she learned how to aim it.

* * *

My best friend ran away with my wife, and let me tell you, I miss him.

* * *

President Reagan met my wife. He declared my home a disaster area!

* * *

My wife is the sweetest, most tolerant, most beautiful woman in the world. This is a paid political announcement.

71

Alimony: Bounty on the Mutiny.

* * *

My wife is a light eater. As soon as it's light she starts eating.

* * *

I said to my wife, "Where do you want to go for your anniversary?"
She said, "I want to go somewhere I've never been before."
I said, "Try the kitchen."

* * *

My wife Sadie just had plastic surgery. I cut up her credit cards.

* * *

My wife was at the beauty shop for two hours, and that was just for the estimate.

* * *

One guy came home and said to his wife, "Someone showed me an amazing device that sews buttons right on clothes."
His wife said, "That's wonderful. What is it?"
And the guy said, "A needle and thread."

We went for a ride, and my wife went through a red light. I said, "Didn't you see that red light?"

She said, "So what? You see one red light, you've seen them all."

* * *

At our country club, one of the members dropped dead. Nobody wanted to tell his wife, so the doctor said he'd do it. He called and said, "Mrs. Cohen, your husband Sam lost $500 playing cards at the club."

* * *

The wife yelled, "He should drop dead."
The doctor said, "He did."

* * *

My wife wanted her face lifted. They couldn't do that. But for $80 they lowered her body.

* * *

A couple is driving to Miami Beach in a brand new car. As they're driving, he puts his hand on her knee. She says, "We're married now, you can go a little further." So he went to Ft. Lauderdale.

My wife always complains about something. She always complains about the housework. So I went out and bought her an electric iron, an electric dishwasher, an electric dryer. She complained: too many gadgets. She had no place to sit down. What did I do to make her happy?

I went out and bought her an electric chair.

* * *

My wife came out to Las Vegas with me. Where do you think she was gambling?

She was playing the stamp machine.

* * *

I came home last night, by accident, and there's the car in the dining room. I said to my wife, "How did you get the car in the dining room?"

She said, "It was easy. I made a left turn when I came out of the kitchen."

* * *

My wife wanted a white mink coat. I told her I'd buy her a white mink when a man walked on the moon. My luck!

Some people ask the secret of our long marriage. We take time to go to a restaurant two times a week. A little candlelight, dinner, soft music and dancing. She goes Tuesdays; I go Fridays.

* * *

My wife put her hand out the car window and signaled right, then left, then she erased it. I said, "What kind of signal is that?"

She said, "I wanted to go right, then I wanted to go left, then I changed my mind. I rubbed it out."

* * *

I'm just back from a pleasure trip. Took my mother-in-law to the airport.

* * *

A woman who never gets taken anywhere by her husband. She says, "What would it take for you to go on a second honeymoon?"

He says, "A second wife!"

We've been married 50 years. Went back to the same hotel where we got married, had the same suite of rooms, only this time *I* went in the bathroom and cried.

*   *   *

My wife has already informed me she doesn't want me to be president. Says she couldn't stand having all the neighbors know exactly what I make.

*   *   *

I don't mind my wife giving me all those TV dinners, but when she starts heating up the leftovers and calling them re-runs . . .

*   *   *

So these two fathers-to-be are pacing the waiting room of a maternity hospital. Suddenly, one starts grumbling. "Don't I have all the luck? This has to happen on my vacation!"

And the other says, "You're complaining. This is our honeymoon!"

I don't know what to do with my wife. Yesterday she was cleaning out the attic and found a case of seventeen-year-old Scotch. So she threw it out. Figured it was stale.

* * *

Many an architect has discovered after the honeymoon that his wife could make plans too.

* * *

Lady
Luck

5.

LADY LUCK

A terrible accident happened to me on the way to the racetrack. I got there safely.

* * *

One day I played a horse so slow the jockey kept a diary of the trip.

* * *

The jockey hit the horse. The horse said, "What are you hitting me for, there's nobody behind us."

* * *

That's the first time I ever saw a horse start from a kneeling position.

81

In Las Vegas, a guy running up and down putting money in parking meters. He says, "I love this outdoor gambling!"

In Las Vegas, a man said to his wife, "Give me the money I told you not to give me."

* * *

I have property in Las Vegas. Caesar's Palace has my luggage.

* * *

A man went to Las Vegas in a $7,000 Cadillac and came home in a $75,000 bus.

* * *

Some people play a horse to win, some to place. I should have bet this horse to live.

* * *

I bet on a great horse. It took nine horses to beat him.

* * *

Strip poker is the only game where the more you lose, the more you have to show for it.

I would have had a wonderful time in Las Vegas if it wasn't for the temperature. The sun was too hot and the dice were too cold.

*　*　*

You can't really call Las Vegas a city. It's more like a garbage disposal for money.

*　*　*

... And More

6.

. . . AND MORE!

A guy says to me, "Do you know where Central Park is?"

I said "No."

He says, "O.K., I'll mug you here."

* * *

I've got a great doctor. He gave a guy six months to live. They couldn't pay his bill so he gave him another six months.

* * *

Somebody asked me, "Henny, do you like bathing beauties?"

I said, "I don't know. I never bathed one."

* * *

You can imagine how much money I have. My banker knocked on my door and asked for his calendar back.

A guy driving in Beverly Hills with a Ford. A crowd yelled, "Yankee, go home!"

* * *

I got a brother-in-law—I don't say he's a thief—he finds things before people lose them.

* * *

Banker is swimming in the water. A shark comes toward him and veers away: professional courtesy!

* * *

One night at a night club, we had only one customer, we made money. We rolled him.

* * *

Nothing confuses a man more who is driving behind a woman who does everything right.

* * *

A doctor advises his patient to stop smoking. He says, "As long as you're quitting, I'll give you $5 for your gold lighter."

When you go in a restaurant always ask for a table near a waiter.

* * *

A guy says to a doctor, "My foot hurts, what will I do for it?"
"Limp."

* * *

My doctor says I must give up those little intimate dinners for two unless I have someone eating with me.

* * *

I said to a guy, "Do you know where Broadway is?"
He said, "Yes," and walked away.

* * *

When you forget someone's name, say "I forgot your first and last name."

* * *

There are so many dirty pictures on Broadway. A guy says to me, "Psst, want to see a clean movie?"

I saw a picket with an empty sign. I said, "What's the idea?"

He says, "I'm looking for a sponsor."

This guy gets loaded with liquor, they make him take the freight elevator.

* * *

If there's a nip in the air he tries to drink it.

* * *

Am I rich?
Why, my bank account is named after me.

* * *

I was so ugly when I was born the doctor slapped my mother.

* * *

They were going to put out a Nixon stamp, but they stopped; people were spitting on the wrong side.

* * *

I just redecorated my bar. I put new drunks around it.

* * *

I solved the parking problem. I bought a parked car.

My brother has a steady job. He's a picket.

* * *

My brother, Lester, is a loser. He just opened a tall man's shop in Tokyo.

* * *

A Hollywood couple got divorced, then they got remarried. The divorce didn't work out.

* * *

We are so rich, we have a Persian rug made out of real Persians.

* * *

New York is so crowded, to get over on the other side of the street, you have to be born there.

* * *

Auto traffic was so heavy it was bumper to bumper. A man pushed a cigarette lighter in, and the woman in the car in front said, "Ouch!"

* * *

A doctor gave me a flu shot, and I got it.

A furrier crossed a mink and a gorilla. Beautiful fur coat, but the sleeves are too long.

I flew out to California, got the flu, and flew back.

*　*　*

Doctor leaving his crowded office to go out to move his car said to his patients, "Don't anybody get better, I'll be right back."

*　*　*

I'll never forget when I lost my baby teeth. I didn't know my father could hit that hard.

*　*　*

If you don't like the way women drive, get off the sidewalk.

*　*　*

I'll never forget my first words in the theatre. "Peanuts, Popcorn!"

*　*　*

My grandson traveled with us. First two words he spoke were, "Room service."

*　*　*

I know a girl who just got an obscene phone call for her girlfriend—collect!

Am I forgetful? Last night I forgot the Alamo.

* * *

Columbus's birthday. I forgot to give him a gift.

* * *

Cancer stops smoking.

* * *

I asked my brother-in-law why he was wearing my raincoat.

"You wouldn't want me to get your suit wet, would you?"

* * *

God sneezed. What could I say to him?

* * *

I like to work in New York rather than in California. I get paid three hours earlier.

* * *

My doctor put his hand on my wallet and said, "Cough."

Guy to a psychiatrist: "Nobody talks to me."

Psychiatrist says, "Next!"

Psychiatrist to patient, says, "What do you do for a living?"

The guy says, "I'm an auto mechanic."

Psychiatrist says, "Get under the couch."

A very exclusive hotel. Room service has an unlisted number.

*   *   *

Doctor said to a little old man, "You're going to live until you're sixty."
He said, "I am sixty."
Doctor said, "What did I tell you?"

*   *   *

My doctor examined this little old lady and told her, "Madam, that is the ugliest body I have ever seen."
She says, "Frankly that's what my doctor told me."
He says, "What did you come to me for?"
"I wanted another opinion."

*   *   *

My violin is very valuable. It's a Sears Yamaha!

*   *   *

Did you hear about the scientist who crossed a praying mantis with a termite, and how he has a bug that says grace before it eats your house.

I was in the supermarket the other day. I thought I was in church. Women were walking up the aisles saying, "Oh, my God!"

* * *

A drunk falls down an empty elevator shaft. He's laying there bleeding. He says, "I said up!"

* * *

My doctor is an eye, ear, nose, and throat and wallet specialist.

* * *

I signed a five-year contract with Buick. I bought a car on time.

* * *

Two guys were talking. What's the latest dope on Wall Street? My son!

* * *

I made a killing in the market. I shot my broker!

A guy says he hasn't had a bite in two days. So I bit him!

* * *

He just got a new job. He's a lifeguard in a car wash.

* * *

Two dumb guys go bear hunting. They see a sign saying, "Bear left," so they went home.

* * *

All the other comedians are in TV. I'm waiting for color radio.

* * *

A fellow walked into a bank. He said, "Give me all your money!" Then, "This is my first hold-up in this bank, don't I get a blender?"

* * *

A fellow walks into a bank and says, "Give me all your money."

Manager says, "take the books too, I'm $10,000 short!"

Want to have some fun?

Walk into an antique shop and say, "What's new?"

* * *

My cousin was in show business. He was a psychic. He knew the exact day he was going to die. The warden told him!

* * *

A woman said, "Henny take weight off. Go to Jack LaLanne or Vic Tanney. They take weight off with their equipment and it works."

A friend of mine went there and took 20 pounds off in one week. Machine took his leg off!

* * *

The plane was going up and down and sideways. A little old lady got nervous. She shouted, "Everybody on the plane pray."

So a man said, "I don't know how to pray."

She said, "Well do something religious."

So he started a bingo game.

* * *

You know what's embarrassing? When you look through a keyhole and see another eye.

I was in the lobby of the Sheraton Hotel and I found a man's hand in my pocket. I said, "What do you want?"

He said, "I want a match."

I said, "Why don't you ask for it?"

He said, "I don't talk to strangers."

*　*　*

One year my brother went into the breeding business. He tried to cross a rooster with a rooster. You know what he got? A very cross rooster!

*　*　*

This weather gets you nuts. One day it's cold, the next day it's hot; I don't know what to hock any more.

*　*　*

. My father was never home, he was always away drinking booze. He saw a sign saying, "Drink Canada Dry!" So he went up there.

*　*　*

Want to have some real laughs? Go to your neighbor's house, go into the bathroom, lock the door, run a quarter of a tub of hot water, and throw in twenty boxes of jello.

He didn't ask me to leave home. He took me down to the highway and pointed.

*　*　*

I feel good today; I was up at the crack of six this morning. Took a brisk walk to the bathroom and was back in bed at 6:05.

*　*　*

A panhandler said to me, "Mister, I haven't tasted food for a week."
I said, "Don't worry, it still tastes the same."

*　*　*

Know what I got for Father's Day?
The bills from Mother's Day.

*　*　*

I have 3 brothers-in-law. One brother-in-law is so smart that during the garbage strike, do you know how he got rid of it? Gift-wrapped it, put it in the back of his car, and they stole it.

*　*　*

My third brother-in-law tells people he's a diamond cutter. He mows the lawn at Yankee Stadium.

What a hotel: the towels were so big and fluffy you could hardly close your suitcase.

Second brother-in-law is an idiot: had a black-out in New York. He was stuck on an escalator for four hours. I asked him, "Why didn't you walk down?"

He said, "I was on my way up."

* * *

The other day a policeman stopped me going the wrong way on a one-way street. "Didn't you see the arrow?"

"Arrow? Honest, Officer, I didn't even see the Indians."

* * *

Would you believe it, I used to play at Carnegie Hall . . . till the cops chased me away.

* * *

A panhandler says, "I haven't eaten in two days."

I said, "Force yourself!"

* * *

A woman called the Police Department and said, "I have a sex maniac in my apartment. Pick him up in the morning."

I know a guy that was so active that five years after he died, his self-winding watch was still running.

* * *

Have you tried vodka and carrot juice?
You get drunk just as fast, but your eyesight gets better.

* * *

Jack the Ripper was never killed. I think he's doing my shirts!

* * *

Income tax. That's the government's version of instant poverty.

* * *

I just finished filling out my income tax form. Who said you can't get wounded by a blank?

* * *

A woman used to go to a doctor to see if she could have children. Now she goes to the landlord.

Two drunks walking along Broadway in New York. One goes down into the subway by mistake. Came up the other entrance and his friend is waiting for him. The waiting drunk says, "Where were you?"

The other one says, "I was in some guy's basement. Has he got a set of trains."

* * *

I saw a funny thing in Miami today. I saw a woman with a cloth coat.

* * *

We got a new garbage disposal: my brother-in-law. He'll eat anything.

* * *

Whistler's mother was doing a handstand. Her son asked, "What's the matter, Ma? You off your rocker?"

* * *

I just heard from Bill Bailey. He's not coming home.

* * *

I once wanted to become an atheist, but I gave up. They have no holidays.

A woman is taking a shower. All of a sudden her doorbell rings. She yells, "Who's there?"

He says, "Blind man."

Well, she's a charitable lady. She runs out of the shower naked and opens the door.

He says, "Where should I put these blinds, lady?"

* * *

One fellow put a gun in my back. He said, "Stick 'em up."

I said, "Stick what up?"

He said, "Don't mix me up. This is my first job."

* * *

Business was so bad the other night the orchestra was playing "Tea for One."

* * *

A guy says to a doctor, "I'm having trouble with my love life at home."

The doctor says, "Take off 20 pounds and run 10 miles a day for two weeks."

Two weeks later, the guy calls the doctor. "Doctor, I took off 20 pounds and I've been running 10 miles a day."

"How is your love life now?"

"I don't know, I'm 140 miles away!"

Did you hear about the near-sighted snake?
He fell in love with a piece of rope!

Baseball. A friend gave me seats for the World Series. From where I sat the game was a rumor. I was up so high the usher stopped halfway; he had a nosebleed. I said to the guy next to me, "What a game."

He said, "What game? I'm flying the mail to Pittsburgh."

* * *

A little old lady walked up to a cop and said, "I was attacked. I was attacked!"

He said, "When?"

She said, "Twenty years ago."

He said, "What are you telling me now for?"

She said, "I like to talk about it once in awhile."

* * *

Americans are getting stronger. Twenty years ago it took two people to carry ten dollars' worth of groceries. Today a five-year-old can do it.

* * *

I went up to visit the doctor with my sore foot. He said, "I'll have you walking in an hour." He did. He stole my car.

116

A lot of people are desperate today. A fellow walked up to me and said, "You see a cop around here?"

I said, "No."

He said, "Stick 'em up!"

* * *

A rich guy in Dallas bought his kid a chemistry outfit: DuPont.

* * *

I don't want to say my grandson eats fast, but he has racing colors on his knife and fork.

* * *

We asked a zoologist how porcupines have sex. "Carefully, very carefully."

* * *

My mother was 88 years old. She never used glasses. Drank right out of the bottle!

* * *

A woman driver hit a guy and knocked him six feet in the air. Then she sued him for leaving the scene of the accident.

In New York's Garment District, a little old man was hit by a car. While waiting for an ambulance, the policeman tucked a blanket under the guy's chin and asked, "Are you comfortable?"

The man said, "I make a nice living."

* * *

Football. A guy told two thieves to steal a jet. They came back with Joe Namath.

* * *

I still love the oldie about the convict who was going to the electric chair and called his lawyer for some advice. The barrister replied, "Don't sit down!"

* * *

A woman wrapped herself in Saran Wrap to take weight off. Her husband comes home, sees her, and says, "Left-overs again!"

* * *

I need you like Telly Savalas needs Head 'n Shoulders.

A "peeping Tom" is a guy who is too lazy to go to the beach.

*　*　*

When Guy Lombardo died, he took New Year's Eve with him.

*　*　*

Mrs. Ponce de Leon says to her husband, "Ponce, you're going to Miami without me!"

*　*　*

What do you have for a sick florist?

*　*　*

Taxi driver to man, "Get out of the cab."
Man says, "What for?"
Taxi driver says, "I don't want anybody behind me when I'm driving."

*　*　*

A man brags about his new hearing aid. "It's the most expensive one I've ever had; it cost $2,500."
His friend asks, "What kind is it?"
He says, "Half-past-four!"

Two kangaroos were talking to each other, and one said, "Gee, I hope it doesn't rain today. I just hate it when the children play inside."

This guy dies and leaves the shortest will. It said, "Being in my sound mind, I spent my money!"

* * *

A doctor asked his woman patient, "Do you know what the most effective birth control pill is?"

She replied, "No."

He said, "That's it!"

* * *

I think there's a lot more truthfulness in advertising than there used to be.

Two weeks ago I bought one of those collapsible swimming pools for the kids. This morning it did.

* * *

The draft board wanted to put me in the Air Force. The Air Force! I get dizzy when my barber pumps the chair too high!

* * *

As the Honorable Senator from Texas once put it, "When those Eskimos convinced Congress to make Alaska the 49th state the American people got the biggest snow job in history!"

Most Texans don't exactly believe in Heaven and Hell. When they die, they figure they either go to Dallas or Alaska.

* * *

Nervous? This boy is half-man; half-Miltown.

* * *

Personally, I felt a lot more safe and secure back in 1933, when all I had to fear was fear itself.

* * *

I just had a wonderful dream. I dreamed the Joneses were trying to keep up with me!

* * *

They're just one of those incompatible couples. He's on Miltown and she's on Benzedrine.

* * *

You know what the Pentagon is. That's the big building in Washington that has five sides . . . on almost every issue.

What a car! I'm gonna call it "Flattery" 'cause it gets me nowhere!

* * *

It's just wonderful, the generosity of Americans. I know one outfit that's already collected $3,000,000, and they don't even have a disease yet.

* * *

Everything's changing. Remember when kids asked you to tuck them in at night? Now they've all got electric blankets. You have to plug them in!

* * *

Have you noticed how many more twins are being born than ever before?
I think the kids are getting afraid to come into this world alone.

* * *

For Christmas I gave my kid a chemistry set and now I'm getting worried. The last time I tried to spank him, he held up a vial and yelled: "Lay one finger on me and we'll all go up together!"

I've got a Christmas toy that's gonna make me a fortune. When the kids are through playing, it puts itself away!

* * *

Have you noticed that most people who give up smoking substitute something for it? Irritability!

* * *

Believe me, this cancer scare has got me worried. I won't even go out with cigarette girls any more.

* * *

Do you realize it only took six days to create the world? Just shows you what can be done if you don't take coffee breaks.

* * *

Faculty. The people who get what's left after the football coach receives his salary.

* * *

It's one of those highly ethical colleges that doesn't believe in buying its football players. All it gives them is room, board, and $200 a week toward their textbooks.

I know one football player who's been in college for 13 years. It's kind of a sad story. He can run and he can kick, but he can't pass.

* * *

What a campaign! The Democrats are calling the Republicans crooks, and the Republicans are calling the Democrats crooks. And the funny part of it is, they're both right!

* * *

I didn't believe there was a recession until last week . . . when I saw this Texan buying a Volkswagen on time.

* * *

I guess you heard about the fella who invented an electric car. For three dollars' worth of electricity you can drive it from Los Angeles to New York. There's only one hitch: the $5,000 extension cord.

* * *

I know a pitcher who made over $100,000 last year. Lost nine games out of eleven, hit .067, but he does a helluva Gillette commercial!

It's a funny thing, I always thought baseball was the national pastime. Then I subscribed to *Playboy*.

* * *

How times have changed. Just 20 years ago most of the best seller list would have been mailed in plain white wrappers.

* * *

Did you hear the one about the ministers who formed a bowling team? Called themselves the Holy Rollers?

* * *

I won't say he cheats, but he won't go bowling any more. Who can tilt an alley?

* * *

You might say the show got divided notices. We liked it, but the critics didn't.

* * *

Actually, there are millions of men in this country running for offices, only most of them we don't call politicians. They're known by a different name: "commuters."

I have a very fine doctor. If you can't afford
the operation, he touches up the X-rays.

Here it is election time and once again isn't it amazing at how many wide open spaces there are, entirely surrounded by teeth.

* * *

I understand the Democrats were gonna run a woman for president but she turned it down. Not enough closets in the White House.

* * *

Personally, I'm against political jokes. Too often they get elected to office.

* * *

It's reassuring to see that colleges are putting the emphasis on education again. One school has gotten so strict, it won't even give a football player his letter, unless he can tell which one it is.

* * *

I've been fed so many TV dinners, yesterday I broke out in a test pattern.

* * *

Remember when *"Charge!"* meant the Light Brigade instead of the Diner's Club?

The trouble with girls today is that all they can do is thaw food. Why can't they open cans like their mothers did?

* * *

It must be wonderful to be a doctor. In what other job could you ask a girl to take her clothes off, look her over at your leisure, and then send a bill to her husband?

* * *

There's nothing wrong with our foreign policy that faith, hope, and clarity couldn't cure.

* * *

Personally, I detest gambling. I'm so dead set against gambling, I'll bet you 2 to 1 they'll never legalize it!

* * *

Isn't it amazing the way carts have taken the place of caddies on the golf course? Let's face it. They have three big advantages: They don't cost; they don't criticize; and they don't count.

* * *

If you stop to think about it, life is like that big golf tournament. As soon as you get out of one hole, you start heading for another.

Things were rough when I was a baby. No talcum powder.

I went to my doctor last week and he told me to take a hot bath before retiring. But that's ridiculous. It'll be years before I retire!

* * *

Two bookies were coming out of a church service. One was rapping the other on the head and saying, "How many times have I told you, it's Hallelujah, not Hialeah!"

* * *

Incidentally, there is no truth to the rumor that Conrad Hilton is planning to buy the Leaning Tower of Pisa, convert it into a hotel, and call it "The Tiltin' Hilton!"

* * *

Mixed Emotions: What you have when your kids borrow ten dollars from you to buy Father's Day presents.

* * *

Did you hear the one about the expectant father who wanted to name the baby Oscar 'cause it was his best performance of the year?

That Florida weather is really something. Cold? It got so bad I had to put anti-freeze in my suntan lotion.

* * *

I hear the big food companies are working on a tearless onion, and I think they can do it. They've already given us tasteless bread.

* * *

Internal Revenue Service. The world's most successful mail-order business.

* * *

Believe me, it's getting to the point where you need more brains to make out the income tax forms than to make the income.

* * *

April 15th. The time you count your blessings, just before sending them off to the Internal Revenue Service.

* * *

April 15th. The day when millions of Americans realize they've got an extra person on their payroll: Uncle Sam!

My grandson, 22 years old, keeps complaining about headaches. I've told him 1,000 times, "Larry, when you get out of bed, it's feet first."

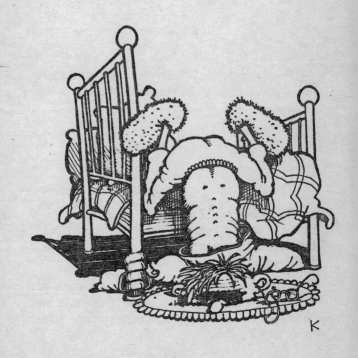

How times have changed. Remember 30 years ago, when a juvenile delinquent was a kid with an overdue library book?

* * *

I'm a little worried about television. The good guys win out on every program but the 11 o'clock news!

* * *

Psychoanalysis. Where you can spend more on a couch than some people do on a six-room house.

* * *

The latest thing in psychiatry is group therapy. Instead of couches, they use bunk beds.

* * *

Have you noticed how all of these rock 'n' roll groups use electric guitars? I don't know what it's doing for music, but it's doing wonders for Con Edison.

138

It's a funny thing. History tells us Lincoln once walked nine miles to borrow a book. So now they close the libraries on his birthday.

* * *

The traffic situation in New York is just impossible. I was telling one cop this morning, "You're giving me a ticket for parking? You should give me a medal!"

* * *

I read about the evils of drinking, so I gave up reading.

* * *

What do you get for a man who has everything?
Penicillin.

* * *

ED MCBAIN'S MYSTERIES

JACK AND THE BEANSTALK   (17-083, $3.95)
Jack's dead, stabbed fourteen times. And thirty-six thousand's missing in cash. Matthew's questions are turning up some long-buried pasts, a second dead body, and some beautiful suspects. Like Sunny, Jack's sister, a surfer boy's fantasy, a delicious girl with some unsavory secrets.

BEAUTY AND THE BEAST   (17-134, $3.95)
She was spectacular—an unforgettable beauty with exquisite features. On Monday, the same woman appeared in Hope's law office to file a complaint. She had been badly beaten—a mass of purple bruises with one eye swollen completely shut. And she wanted her husband put away before something worse happened. Her body was discovered on Tuesday, bound with wire coat hangers and burned to a crisp. But her husband—big, and monstrously ugly—denies the charge.

EDGE by George G. Gilman

#5 BLOOD ON SILVER   (17-225, $3.50)

The Comstock Lode was one of the richest silver strikes the world had ever seen. So Edge was there. So was the Tabor gang—sadistic killers led by a renegade Quaker. The voluptuous Adele Firman, a band of brutal Shoshone Indians, and an African giant were there, too. Too bad. They learned that gold may be warm but silver is death. They didn't live to forget Edge.

#6 RED RIVER   (17-226, $3.50)

In jail for a killing he didn't commit, Edge is puzzled by the prisoner in the next cell. Where had they met before? Was it at Shiloh, or in the horror of Andersonville?

This is the sequel to KILLER'S BREED, an earlier volume in this series. We revisit the bloody days of the Civil War and incredible scenes of cruelty and violence as our young nation splits wide open, blue armies versus gray armies, tainting the land with a river of blood. And Edge was there.

Available wherever paperbacks are sold, or order direct from the Publisher. Send cover price plus 50¢ per copy for mailing and handling to Pinnacle Books, Dept.17-484, 475 Park Avenue South, New York, N.Y. 10016. Residents of New York, New Jersey and Pennsylvania must include sales tax. DO NOT SEND CASH.

WARBOTS by G. Harry Stine

#5 OPERATION HIGH DRAGON   (17-159, $3.95)

Civilization is under attack! A "virus program" has been injected into America's polar-orbit military satellites by an unknown enemy. The only motive can be the preparation for attack against the free world. The source of "infection" is traced to a barren, storm-swept rock-pile in the southern Indian Ocean. Now, it is up to the forces of freedom to search out and destroy the enemy. With the aid of their robot infantry—the Warbots—the Washington Greys mount Operation High Dragon in a climactic battle for the future of the free world.

#6 THE LOST BATTALION   (17-205, $3.95)

Major Curt Carson has his orders to lead his Warbot-equipped Washington Greys in a search-and-destroy mission in the mountain jungles of Borneo. The enemy: a strongly entrenched army of Shiite Muslim guerrillas who have captured the Second Tactical Battalion, threatening them with slaughter. As allies, the Washington Greys have enlisted the Grey Lotus Battalion, a mixed-breed horde of Japanese jungle fighters. Together with their newfound allies, the small band must face swarming hordes of fanatical Shiite guerrillas in a battle that will decide the fate of Southeast Asia and the security of the free world.

#7 OPERATION IRON FIST   (17-253, $3.95)

Russia's centuries-old ambition to conquer lands along its southern border erupts in a savage show of force that pits a horde of Soviet-backed Turkish guerrillas against the freedom-loving Kurds in their homeland high in the Caucasus Mountains. At stake: the rich oil fields of the Middle East. Facing certain annihilation, the valiant Kurds turn to the robot infantry of Major Curt Carson's "Ghost Forces" for help. But the brutal Turks far outnumber Carson's desperately embattled Washington Greys, and on the blood-stained slopes of historic Mount Ararat, the high-tech warriors of tomorrow must face their most awesome challenge yet!

THE EXECUTIONER
by Don Pendleton